Making Sense of Maths

Sorting letters

Paul Dickinson
Stella Dudzic
Frank Eade
Steve Gough
Sue Hough

HODDER
EDUCATION
AN HACHETTE UK COMPANY

The publishers would like to thank the following for permission to reproduce copyright material:

Photo credits: page 1 © Torsten Blackwood/AFP/Getty Images; page 16 © Sandy Officer; page 17 © Kate Crossland-Page; page 22 © Kate Crossland-Page; page 23 t © Caitlin Seymour; page 23 b © Kate Crossland-Page; page 26 © Sue Hough; page 30 © Monkey Business – Fotolia; page 46 *all photos* © Steve Gough; page 49 © djtaylor – Fotolia; page 51 *all photos* © Steve Gough; page 53 *all photos* © Steve Gough.

t = top, c = centre, b = bottom, l = left, r = right

All designated trademarks and brands are protected by their respective trademarks.

Every effort has been made to trace all copyright holders, but if any have been inadvertently overlooked, the Publishers will be pleased to make the necessary arrangements at the first opportunity.

Although every effort has been made to ensure that website addresses are correct at time of going to press, Hodder Education cannot be held responsible for the content of any website mentioned in this book. It is sometimes possible to find a relocated web page by typing in the address of the home page for a website in the URL window of your browser.

Hachette UK's policy is to use papers that are natural, renewable and recyclable products and made from wood grown in sustainable forests. The logging and manufacturing processes are expected to conform to the environmental regulations of the country of origin.

Orders: please contact Bookpoint Ltd, 130 Milton Park, Abingdon, Oxon OX14 4SB. Telephone: (44) 01235 827720. Fax: (44) 01235 400454. Lines are open 9.00–5.00, Monday to Saturday, with a 24-hour message answering service. Visit our website at www.hoddereducation.co.uk

© Paul Dickinson, Stella Dudzic, Frank Eade, Steve Gough and Sue Hough 2013

First published in 2013 by
Hodder Education, an Hachette UK company,
338 Euston Road
London NW1 3BH

Impression number 5 4 3 2 1
Year 2017 2016 2015 2014 2013

Cover photo © Torsten Blackwood/AFP/Getty Images
Illustrations by Integra Software Services Pvt. Ltd., Pondicherry, India
Typeset by Integra Software Services Pvt. Ltd., Pondicherry, India
Printed in Spain

A catalogue record for this title is available from the British Library

ISBN 978 1444 180114

Contents

Introduction   v

Chapter 1: Patterns

■ People patterns   1
■ Different patterns   5
■ Patterns in numbers   9
■ Summary   13

Chapter 2: Formulas in focus

■ What's the temperature?   14
■ Think of a number   18
■ Choosing a plumber   19
■ Taxi charges   22
■ Summary   25

Chapter 3: Equivalent ways of working

■ Clever counting   26
■ Multiplications   29
■ Football pitches   31
■ Seeing multiplication as area   33
■ Perimeter and area   36
■ Expanding and factorising   39
■ Using the 'lots of' strategy   42
■ Using the 'times by' strategy   43
■ Summary   44

Chapter 4: Combinations

■ The honesty box   46

■ Break time   49

■ Pitch and Putt at North Park   51

■ The shop at North Park   52

■ More chocolate!   54

■ Summary   56

Introduction

These books are intended to help you to make sense of the maths you do in school and the maths you need to use outside school. They have already been tried out in classrooms, and are the result of many comments made by the teachers and the students who have used them. Students told us that after working with these materials they were more able to understand the maths they had done, and teachers found that students also did better in tests and examinations.

Most of the time you will be working 'in context' – in other words, in real-life situations that you will either have been in yourself or can imagine being in. For example, in this book you will be looking at ways of counting how many people are needed to form a pattern, as well as comparing temperatures, taxi charges, football pitches and Pitch and Putt prices, among many other things.

You will regularly be asked to 'draw something' – drawings and sketches are very important in maths and often help us to solve problems and to see connections between different topics. In the trials, students found that linking algebra to pictures really helped them to develop meanings which they could understand.

You will also be expected to talk about your maths, explaining your ideas to small groups or to the whole class. We all learn by explaining our own ideas and by listening to and trying out the ideas of others.

Finally, of course, you will be expected to practice solving problems and answering examination questions.

We hope that through working in this way you will come to understand the maths you do, enjoy examination success, and be confident when using your maths outside school.

People patterns

1 At the opening and closing ceremonies of major events such as the Olympics or Commonwealth Games, people are often used to form patterns or to spell out messages.

The picture below is from the closing ceremony of the 2006 Commonwealth Games in Melbourne.

Why do you think it says 'Delhi 2010' in the photograph?

2 The image 'Delhi 2010' was made by local school students in different coloured outfits lying down next to each other. How many students do you think it would take to make this image?

3 Which part of 'Delhi 2010' do you think would be the most difficult to do?

4 When the organisers plan the ceremonies, they usually begin with quite simple images. For example, for one event they began by forming a number of boxes as shown below.

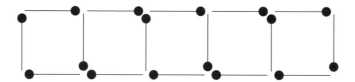

  a) If each small line is one person, how many people will be needed altogether to make this pattern?

  b) Describe carefully how you counted the people and compare your method with those used by others in your class.

5 If you needed to make eight boxes altogether, explain carefully how you would organise the people and in what order you would get them to lie down.

6 How many people are needed altogether for eight boxes?

7 Ben and Sanjay, two of the organisers, are discussing how to work out how many people are needed to make different numbers of boxes.

Once I know that it takes 16 people to make 5 boxes, it's obvious that it must take 32 people to make 10 boxes.

Sanjay

I disagree, Ben. I think it only takes 31 people to make 10 boxes.

Ben

Who is right? Draw a diagram to help you explain how the mistake has been made.

8 How many people will it take to make 20 boxes?

9 Ben decides to make up a table to show him how many people will be
needed for different numbers of boxes. So far, his table looks like this:

Number of boxes	Number of people
1	4
2	7
3	
4	
5	16
6	
7	
8	
9	
10	31

Copy and complete Ben's table.

10 How could you use the table to work out the number of people needed to
make 20 boxes?

11 Work out the number of people needed to make:
a) 14 boxes
b) 23 boxes

12 Suzanne is the overall organiser of the ceremony. She needs to know how to work out how many people are needed to make different numbers of boxes. She asks Sanjay and Ben to help.

Ben says:

It's easy, you just add 3 on each time.

Ben

Suzanne

Ben gives Suzanne a piece of paper with this on it:

rule is $+3$

Sanjay says:

The number of people is 3 times the number of boxes plus 1. It's like the 3 times table add 1.

And on his piece of paper he writes:

rule is

$3n + 1$

Sanjay

Explain carefully why, even though they have written different things, Sanjay and Ben are both correct.

13 Suzanne actually wants enough people to create 36 boxes.
   a) How many people are needed?
   b) Is it easier to use Ben's or Sanjay's method to work this out?

14 There is a problem! Only 100 people are available.
   a) What is the largest number of boxes that can be made?
   b) Will this number use all 100 people, or will some people not be used?

Different patterns

15 In another part of the ceremony, people are going to form rectangular boxes like this:

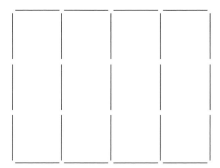

How many people are needed for the four boxes shown above?

16 Is this way of making boxes going to use more or fewer people than the square boxes made earlier?

17 The following table shows the number of people needed to make different numbers of rectangular boxes.

Number of boxes	Number of people
1	8
2	13
3	18
4	
5	
6	
7	
8	
9	
10	

Complete this table by doing **Workbook exercise 1.1** on page 1 of your workbook.

18 Ben says:

Ben

To work out how many people you need, you just keep adding 5.

Suzanne

He gives Suzanne a piece of paper with '+5' written on it.

Sanjay says:

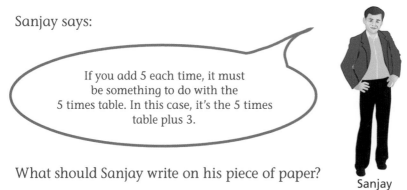

If you add 5 each time, it must be something to do with the 5 times table. In this case, it's the 5 times table plus 3.

What should Sanjay write on his piece of paper?

Sanjay

19 Suzanne says:

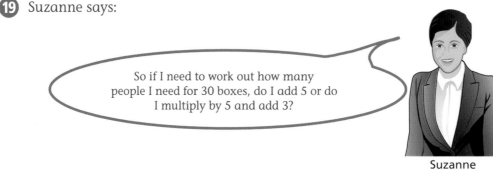

So if I need to work out how many people I need for 30 boxes, do I add 5 or do I multiply by 5 and add 3?

Suzanne

How should Suzanne work out how many people are needed for 30 boxes?

20 If only 100 people were available, how many boxes could be made? How many people would be left over?

Now complete Workbook exercise 1.2 on pages 2–5 of your workbook.

21 For other parts of the ceremony, shapes other than rectangles are needed. Suzanne gives Ben and Sanjay a drawing to show some of the other arrangements she would like to make. In each case, she wants to know how to work out how many people are needed for different numbers of the shapes. The drawing Suzanne gives them looks like this:

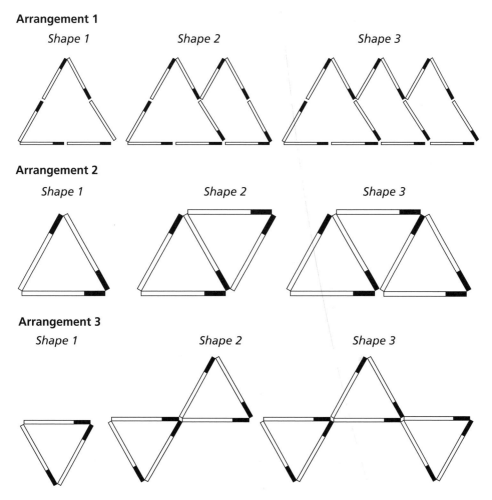

Arrangement 1
Shape 1   *Shape 2*   *Shape 3*

Arrangement 2
Shape 1   *Shape 2*   *Shape 3*

Arrangement 3
Shape 1   *Shape 2*   *Shape 3*

For Arrangement 1, draw what the fifth shape would look like. Then copy and complete the following table.

Shape number (term)	Number of people needed
1	6
2	10
3	14
4	
5	

22 For Arrangement 2, make a drawing of the fifth shape and then make a table for the first five shapes.

23 Repeat this for Arrangement 3.

24 Sanjay says: 'I can see straight away that the rule for Arrangement 1 is connected to the 4 times table, the rule for Arrangement 2 is connected to the 2 times table, and the rule for Arrangement 3 is connected to the 3 times table. I can tell this from the drawing *or* from the table.'

   a) Explain **using the drawing** how Sanjay knows that the rule for Arrangement 1 is connected to the 4 times table.

   b) Explain **using the table** how Sanjay knows that the rule for Arrangement 2 is connected to the 2 times table.

25 For Arrangement 1, Sanjay works out that the rule is the 4 times table plus 2. He writes down: $4n + 2$.

   What would Sanjay write down as the rule for Arrangement 3?

> Sanjay's rule is usually called
> the nth term.

26 What would be the nth term for Arrangement 2?

27 Suzanne has provisionally booked 600 children for the ceremony. For each of the three arrangements on page 7, work out the biggest complete pattern she could make using these children.

28 The final 'people arrangement' used at the ceremony uses the rule $5n + 3$ to work out how many people are needed.

   a) How many people will be needed for the eighth shape in this arrangement?

   b) If Suzanne uses this arrangement, will she be able to use all 600 children? Explain carefully how you worked out your answer.

Patterns in numbers

29 A group of students were asked to display a number sequence of their choice on a 100 square. Below is a record of what they produced.

a)

1	2	3	4	5	6	7	8	(9)	10
11	12	13	14	15	16	(17)	18	19	20
21	22	23	24	(25)	26	27	28	29	30
31	32	(33)	34	35	36	37	38	39	40
(41)	42	43	44	45	46	47	48	(49)	50
51	52	53	54	55	56	(57)	58	59	60
61	62	63	64	(65)	66	67	68	69	70
71	72	(73)	74	75	76	77	78	79	80
(81)	82	83	84	85	86	87	88	(89)	90
91	92	93	94	95	96	(97)	98	99	100

b)

1	2	3	4	5	6	(7)	8	9	10
11	(12)	13	14	15	16	(17)	18	19	20
21	(22)	23	24	25	26	(27)	28	29	30
31	(32)	33	34	35	36	(37)	38	39	40
41	(42)	43	44	45	46	(47)	48	49	50
51	(52)	53	54	55	56	(57)	58	59	60
61	(62)	63	64	65	66	(67)	68	69	70
71	(72)	73	74	75	76	(77)	78	79	80
81	(82)	83	84	85	86	(87)	88	89	90
91	(92)	93	94	95	96	(97)	98	99	100

c)

(1)	2	(3)	4	(5)	6	(7)	8	(9)	10
(11)	12	(13)	14	(15)	16	(17)	18	(19)	20
(21)	22	(23)	24	(25)	26	(27)	28	(29)	30
(31)	32	(33)	34	(35)	36	(37)	38	(39)	40
(41)	42	(43)	44	(45)	46	(47)	48	(49)	50
(51)	52	(53)	54	(55)	56	(57)	58	(59)	60
(61)	62	(63)	64	(65)	66	(67)	68	(69)	70
(71)	72	(73)	74	(75)	76	(77)	78	(79)	80
(81)	82	(83)	84	(85)	86	(87)	88	(89)	90
(91)	92	(93)	94	(95)	96	(97)	98	(99)	100

d)

1	2	3	4	5	6	7	8	9	10
11	12	13	14	15	(16)	17	18	19	20
21	(22)	23	24	25	26	27	(28)	29	30
31	32	33	(34)	35	36	37	38	39	(40)
41	42	43	44	45	(46)	47	48	49	50
51	(52)	53	54	55	56	57	(58)	59	60
61	62	63	(64)	65	66	67	68	69	(70)
71	72	73	74	75	(76)	77	78	79	80
81	(82)	83	84	85	86	87	(88)	89	90
91	92	93	(94)	95	96	97	98	99	(100)

In each case, write a rule for the *n*th term in the sequence.

30 Below is a dot pattern and also a table to go with it.

Term: 1   2   3   4

Dot
pattern:

Term	Number of dots
1	1
2	4
3	
4	
5	
6	

Draw the next two patterns in the sequence, and then copy and complete the table.

31 Work out the rule for this sequence and explain carefully how you found your answer.

32 Tarik's teacher asked him to make up a dot pattern of his own. The rule Tarik used was $3n + 2$.

a) Make up a table to show the first six terms in Tarik's sequence.

b) Draw a dot pattern to show the first six terms in Tarik's sequence.

33 Draw a dot pattern for the rule $2n - 1$.
Compare your drawing with those of other people in your class.

 Now do Workbook exercise 1.3 on pages 6–8 of your workbook.

34 Look at the sequence of numbers below:

1
1 + 3
1 + 3 + 5
1 + 3 + 5 + 7

a) What kind of numbers are being added together here?

b) Write down the next two terms in the sequence.

35 Sometimes it helps to draw a picture of a number pattern. For the pattern in **question 34**, Katy draws:

Term:	1	2	3
Pattern:			
Total number of dots:	1	4	9

a) Explain why you think Katy has used different colours.

b) Draw the next two patterns in this sequence.

c) How many dots would you need to draw the 10th pattern in this sequence?

d) Make a list of the number of dots needed to make each of the first 10 patterns in this sequence. What do we call these numbers?

e) Is 200 a square number? Explain carefully how you got your answer.

f) Write down the nth term of this sequence.

36 Tarik is working with a different sequence of numbers. His sequence begins:

1
1 + 2
1 + 2 + 3

He draws:

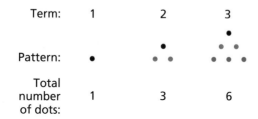

Term:	1	2	3
Pattern:	•		
Total number of dots:	1	3	6

a) Draw the next two patterns in this sequence and write down the number of dots in each pattern.

b) Look at the pattern the dots are making. What name would you give to the numbers 1, 3, 6, 10, 15... etc.?

c) Tarik says that the rule for working out how many dots are needed in the pattern is $\dfrac{n(n + 1)}{2}$. He works out that 45 dots will be needed for the 9th pattern. Explain carefully how Tarik got his answer of 45.

d) How would you work out how many dots were needed for the 20th pattern?

e) How many dots would be needed altogether if there were seven dots across the base?

Now do Workbook exercise 1.4 on pages 9–11 of your workbook.

Summary

This chapter has been concerned with drawing and generalising patterns. A pattern may be shown as a set of drawings, in a table, or simply as a sequence of numbers.

For example:

Drawing

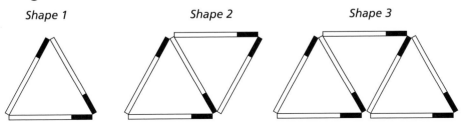

Shape 1   Shape 2   Shape 3

Table

Shape number (term)	Number of people needed
1	3
2	5
3	7
4	
5	

Sequence

3, 5, 7...

In most of the patterns, we add the same amount on each time, which means that the numbers have some connection to a multiplication table.

In the example above, we are adding 2 on each time, so this must be something to do with the two times table. In this case, the numbers are the two times table with one added on. We write this as **$2n + 1$**.

We say that $2n + 1$ is the **general term** or the **nth term** of the sequence.

What's the temperature?

1 Steve and his Grandad are planning a trip to London on Monday. They want to know what the weather will be like, so that they know what clothes to pack. You can see the website pages that they looked at below.

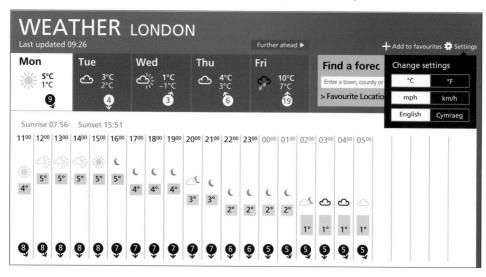

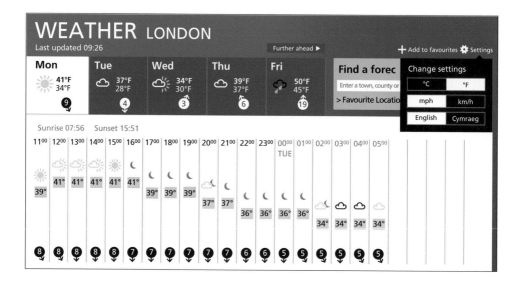

a) What is the same about these web pages and what is different about them?

b) Steve used one of the pages, his Grandad used another. Who do you think used which page?

On the day they were looking at this, the temperature was actually 10 °C.

It's going to get colder when we're away. It's actually 10 degrees Celsius today.

What's that in my sort of temperatures?

c) Roughly what would 10 °C be in degrees Fahrenheit?

d) Estimate the following temperatures:
- **i)** Today's temperature
- **ii)** Your bath temperature
- **iii)** The temperature of your local swimming baths
- **iv)** The cold tap temperature
- **v)** The temperature used to cook oven chips
- **vi)** The temperature of ice

2 A formula which is quite good for converting temperatures is given by:

$$F = 2C + 30$$

a) Say this formula in words.

b) Use this formula to change 10 °C to Fahrenheit and compare your answer with the one you got in **question 1**.

c) Use this formula to convert your estimated temperatures for **question 1 d)**.

3 If the temperature was 16 °C, what would this be in Fahrenheit?

4 In Spain in the summer months, the daytime temperature is about 35 °C. What is this in Fahrenheit?

5 We might also need to convert temperatures from Fahrenheit to Celsius using this formula.

76 °F would be a nice warm summer temperature.

Try to work out what 76 °F would be in degrees Celsius.

6 Andy and Jane are discussing how they worked out their answers in **question 5**.

Andy writes:

$$F = 2C + 30$$

$$76 = 2C + 30$$

$$46 = 2C$$

$$23 = C$$

This is a little like solving equations. I did the same to both sides.

a) Explain carefully how Andy got '46'.
b) Explain carefully how Andy got '23'.

7

I have loads of these to do, so I've rearranged the formula first. I used 'do the same to both sides' like when we were solving equations.

Jane writes:

$$F = 2C + 30$$

$$F - 30 = 2C$$

$$\frac{F - 30}{2} = C$$

a) Explain carefully what Jane has done on each line.

b) Use Jane's new formula to work out what 76 °F would be in degrees Celsius.

8 Andy sees this as using a flow chart method. He writes:

Start with C → ×2 → +30 → get F

get C ← ÷2 ← −30 ← Start with F

So $C = \dfrac{F - 30}{2}$

Explain clearly how Andy got his answer.

This is called **making C the subject of the formula**.

9 **a)** 40°F would be quite a cold winter temperature. What would this be in degrees Celsius?

b) What is 90°F in degrees Celsius?

Think of a number

10 In the car on the way to London Steve and his Grandad play 'Think of a number'.

Steve starts: 'I think of a number, double it, add 4 and I get 22.'
His Grandad says: 'That's easy, your number must be 9.'

They take it in turns to play this game and try to make the questions more challenging each time.

a) Solve as many of their puzzles as you can.
   i) 'I think of a number, add 10, times by 3 and I get 45.'
   ii) 'I think of a number, add 6, times by 2, add 4 and I get 24.'
   iii) 'I think of a number, take away 5, times by 4 and I get 12.'
   iv) 'I think of a number, times by 5, times by 2, add 50 and I get 150.'
   v) 'I think of a number, divide it by 6 and I get 5.'
   vi) 'I think of a number, divide it by 3, add 4 and I get 10.'
   vii) 'I think of a number, times by 10, add 3, times by 2, take away 1 and I get 45.'
   viii) 'I think of a number, divide by 2, add 10, times by 2 and I get 26.'

b) Now try using the flow chart method to solve the last two puzzles.

c) Make up three 'Think of a number' puzzles for your partner to solve.

11 In the following puzzles, ? stands for a missing number.

i)	$? + 11 = 20$	**ii)**	$2(?) + 6 = 36$
iii)	$? - 17 = 31$	**iv)**	$16 = ? + 9$
v)	$32 = 3(?) + 5$	**vi)**	$5(?) - 12 = 23$
vii)	$2(?) - 3 = 12$	**viii)**	$\frac{1}{2}(?) = 50$
ix)	$\frac{1}{2}(?) + 11 = 21$	**x)**	$(?)^2 = 49$
xi)	$3(? + 5) = 27$	**xii)**	$4(? - 3) + 2 = 30$

a) Say each puzzle as a 'Think of a number' problem.

b) Solve each puzzle. (If you get stuck try using a flow chart.)

 Now complete Workbook exercise 2.1 on pages 12 and 13 of your workbook.

Choosing a plumber

12 Vicky needs a plumber to come and fix her boiler. She finds a firm called Pedro's Plumbers on the Internet. They advertise their charges as:

> ## £20 call-out charge plus £30 per hour

a) How do these charges compare with any trades-people that you know?

b) Vicky estimates that her boiler will take 3 hours to fix. What will be the total price if she uses Pedro's Plumbers?

c) A friend recommends a different firm called Perfect Pipes. Their charges are £60 call-out plus £25 per hour. Vicky wants to pay as little as possible to get her boiler fixed. Which of the two firms would you advise Vicky to use? Explain your answer carefully.

13 On the Perfect Pipes website, someone has asked how to work out the total price of a job.

One of the answers is:

To work out the total price of a job, you can use a flow chart like this:

Start with number of hours (h) → $\times 25$ → $+60$ → get total price (P)

or you can use the formula $P = 25h + 60$.

a) What does '25h' mean in the formula?

b) Use either method to work out the total price of a job that will take 7 hours.

c) What would be the flow chart and formula that you would use for Pedro's Plumbers?

d) If a job was going to take 5 hours, which of the two firms would be the cheapest to use?

e) Is there a length of job for which the two firms would charge the same amount?

14 When Joe asks Pedro's Plumbers about doing some work in his house, he is told that the total price will be about £350. How many hours work will this be? Explain carefully how you got your answer.

15 Dave works for Perfect Pipes. He says, 'Last week I worked on the same job all week and earned £810.'

a) How many hours did Dave work? Explain carefully how you got your answer.

To work out how many hours he worked in total, Dave writes down the following:

$$h \rightarrow \boxed{\times 25} \rightarrow \boxed{+60} \rightarrow P$$

$$h \leftarrow \boxed{\div 25} \leftarrow \boxed{-60} \leftarrow P$$

$$h = \frac{P - 60}{25}$$

b) Use either the flow chart or the formula to check your answer to **question 14**.

c) Write down the flow chart and equation that would allow Pedro's Plumbers to calculate how many hours they had worked if they knew their total earnings for one job.

16 Almost all plumbers have a call-out charge and an hourly rate. The general way to write the total price for a job would be:

$$P = r\,h + c$$

a) Explain carefully what P, r, h, and c stand for.

b) Copy and complete the following flow chart.

c) Use either the formula or flow chart to work out the total price for a job which lasts 6 hours, if $r = 20$ and $c = 45$.

d) Show how you could rearrange the formula and flow chart to work out h if you knew P, r, and c.

Taxi charges

17 Aneesa wanted to get a taxi to the station and used Metro Cabs. When she got into the taxi, she noticed that the meter was already showing £2. Why do you think this was the case?

18 When Aneesa asked the cab driver how the fare system worked, she said that there was a standard initial charge and then an additional charge per mile. The formula for working out the total charge (T) in £ is given by $T = 2 + 3n$, where n is the number of miles.

a) How much is the standard initial charge?

b) How much is the additional charge per mile?

c) If Aneesa's journey was 5 miles, how much did she pay altogether?

19 On another occasion, Aneesa used a different taxi firm called Yellow Cabs. Their formula for working out the total cost in £ was:

$$T = 5 + 2n$$

a) How much would she pay with Yellow Cabs to do the 5 mile journey to the station?

b) Which of the two firms would it be best to use for a journey of 15 miles?

c) Why does a journey of 15 miles not cost three times as much as a journey of 5 miles?

d) Is there a journey length which would cost the same amount with both taxi companies?

20 Aneesa's brother also used Yellow Cabs for a journey recently, and told Aneesa about it.

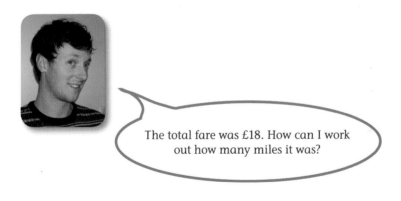

The total fare was £18. How can I work out how many miles it was?

That's easy. You write a flow chart or formula and then rearrange it.

Aneesa writes:

Flowchart

$$n \longrightarrow \boxed{\times 2} \longrightarrow \boxed{+5} \longrightarrow T$$

$$n \longleftarrow \boxed{\div 2} \longleftarrow \boxed{-5} \longleftarrow T$$

$$So \quad \frac{T-5}{2} = n$$

Formula

$$T = 5 + 2n$$

$$T - 5 = 2n$$

$$\frac{T-5}{2} = n$$

a) Use either the flow chart or formula to work out the number of miles of her brother's journey.

b) If Yellow Cabs charged a customer £15, how long was the journey?

c) The original formula for Metro Cabs was $T = 2 + 3n$.
Rearrange this formula to make n the subject.
Write your answer both as a flow chart and a formula.

d) If Metro Cabs charged £17 for a journey, how long was the journey?

 Now complete Workbook exercise 2.2 on pages 14–15 of your workbook.

Summary

In this chapter we have looked at using formulas. In particular, we have substituted numbers into formulas, and also rearranged formulas.

For example, a taxi fare might be worked out using the formula $C = 4 + 2n$, where C is the total cost of the journey in £ and n is the number of miles travelled.

So the cost of a journey of 12 miles would be worked out by $C = 4 + (2 \times 12)$ which would be £28.

If we knew the cost, and wanted to know how many miles we had travelled, we could first of all rearrange the formula. This is the same process as solving equations.

If $C = 4 + 2n$, then $C - 4 = 2n$

So $\dfrac{C - 4}{2} = n$

Here we have made n the subject of the formula.

So if the total cost of the taxi was £20, we could work out how many miles we had travelled by doing

$\dfrac{20 - 4}{2} = 8$

So this was a journey of 8 miles.

Clever counting

1 Helen is a Year 10 GCSE student. During the summer holidays she has to look after her 7-year-old sister. She sets her sister the task of counting all the 2p coins in this box.

Helen is surprised to see that her sister touch-counts every coin.

a) Repeat this process for yourself, touch-counting every coin. Write down the thoughts that come into your head as you do this.

b) What would you suggest to Helen's sister as a way to speed up this process?

2 Below is the work of some 8-year-olds. They were asked to experiment with different ways of counting the number of squares in the grid.

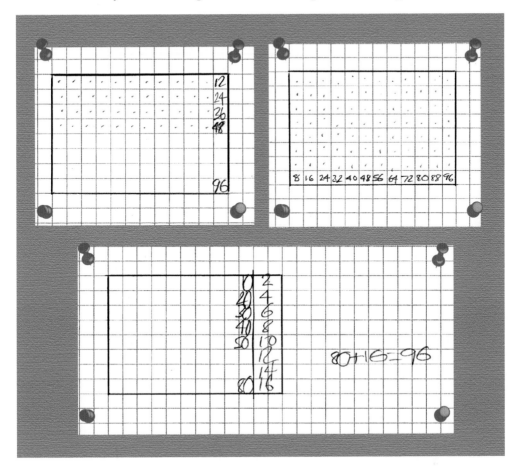

a) Look at the work of each student and describe **exactly** how you think they counted the squares.

b) Who had the most efficient method?

c) Suggest some other ways of counting the squares.

③ A group of Year 9 students were asked to find the number of squares in this grid.

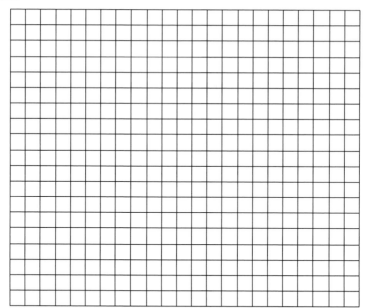

The Year 9 students didn't count all the squares. Instead they did a calculation. You can see their calculations below:

Dez's method

```
  2 3
  1 9
─────
2 3 0
2 0 7
─────
4 3 7
─────
```

Sylvia's method

	20	3
10	200	30
9	180	27

= 437

Nadeem's method

$23 \times 20 = 460$

$460 - 23 = 437$

a) Does it look like there would be 437 squares in the grid if you were to count them?

b) Sylvia has the number 180 in her calculation. Does this refer to some of the squares in the grid? If so, where are they?

 Turn to Workbook exercise 3.1 on pages 16–19 of your workbook and match the students' calculations to the corresponding groups of squares in the grid.

Multiplications

4 Sabir thinks he can do any multiplication by drawing a rectangle and splitting it up into easy-to-count blocks.

His teacher asks him to work out 32 × 56.

Sabir starts by drawing this picture:

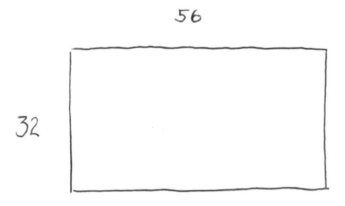

a) Do you think he has drawn his picture to scale or not?

b) Sabir continues as follows:

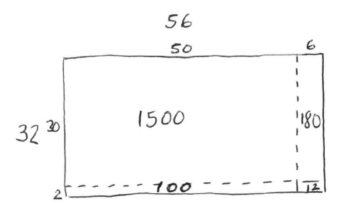

Describe what he has done.

c) Where can you see 32 lots of 56 in Sabir's picture?

d) What is the answer to 32 × 56?

e) Make your own drawings on plain paper and use Sabir's method to work out:

i) 24 × 52   ii) 28 × 61   iii) 36 × 49

iv) 116 × 25   v) 79 × 81   vi) 55 × 274

5 a) Sabir's friend Aaron says he has a different way to work out multiplications. This is what he does to work out 42 × 59:

'I do (40 lots of 50) + (40 lots of 9) + (2 lots of 50) + (2 lots of 9).'

Make a drawing to help you decide whether this will give the right answer or not.

b) Use Aaron's method to work out:

i) 57 × 82

ii) 36 × 49

iii) 41 × 63

iv) 104 × 27

c) Liz says she has a quick way of squaring big numbers:

'If you want to work out, say, 36^2, you square the 30, square the 6 and then add them together.'

Make a drawing to help explain to Liz why her method won't work.

d) Make drawings to help you work out:

i) 25^2

ii) 51^2

iii) 102^2

Football pitches

6 Did you know that not all football pitches are the same size?

    a) Name some pitches that you have played on or seen that you think might be different sizes.

    b) The diagram below shows the possible range of measurements for the size of a pitch.

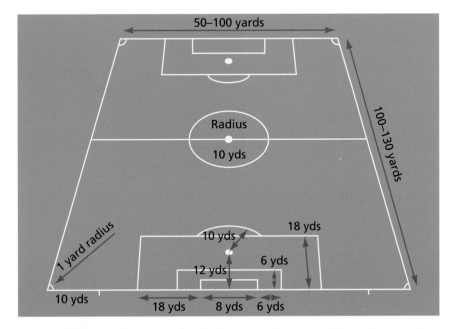

    How much more ground would you have to cover when playing on the largest possible pitch compared with the smallest?

    c) Why do you think there is such a range in the sizes of pitch allowed?

    d) The standard recommended size for a Premier League football pitch is 105 metres (115 yards) long by 68 metres (74 yards) wide. Although many of the Premier League teams follow this guide, there can be variations. In the past some teams have adjusted their pitches depending on who they're playing the following week. Suggest some reasons why teams might do this.

e) Liverpool are due to play Manchester United. The Liverpool manager is talking to his team about how to deal with the extra size of the United pitch compared with their own pitch at Anfield. The United pitch is 6 yards longer and 1 yard wider than the Anfield pitch. The Anfield pitch is 110 yards long by 75 yards wide.

The Liverpool manager draws this sketch on the board.

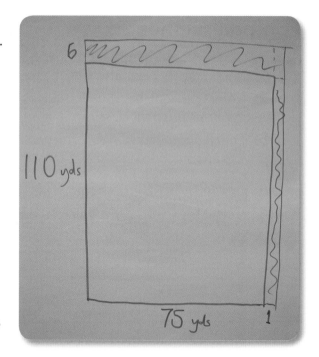

How realistic is his diagram?

f) Copy his diagram (or draw your own version). Use it to work out how much larger the United pitch is than the Liverpool pitch.

g) The table shows how the size of some other Premier League pitches compare with Anfield:

Football stadium	Difference in size compared with Anfield
Villa Park, Aston Villa	5 yards longer, 3 yards shorter in width
Stamford Bridge, Chelsea	3 yards longer, 1 yard shorter in width
Etihad Stadium, Manchester City	6½ yards longer, 2 yards wider
Old Trafford, Manchester United	6 yards longer, 1 yard wider
Upton Park, West Ham	Same length, 5 yards shorter in width

   i) At which football stadium will the Liverpool team have the most extra ground to cover?

   ii) Which ground is the closest in size to Anfield?

Seeing multiplication as area

7 Grace is a Year 9 student who likes to think of maths in pictures. When she sees a multiplication, she draws a rectangle and asks herself how many squares there would be inside the rectangle.

Grace's teacher thinks Grace could use this method to answer more difficult questions. He asks her what she would do for the following questions:

i) 3×187 **ii)** 36×42 **iii)** $2a \times b$ **iv)** $y \times y$
v) $x(x + 2)$ **vi)** $(y + 4)6$ **vi)** $(L + 4)(L + 6)$

Her work is shown below:

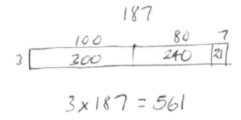

$$3 \times 187 = 561$$

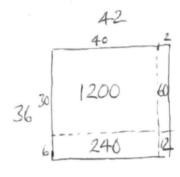

$$36 \times 42 = 1512$$

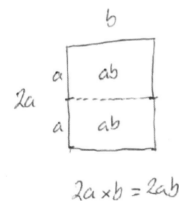

$$2a \times b = 2ab$$

$$y \times y = y^2$$

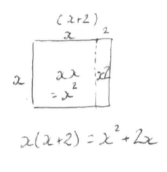

$$x(x+2) = x^2 + 2x$$

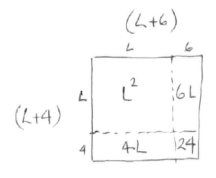

$$(y+4)6 = 6y + 24$$

$$(L+4)(L+6) = L^2 + 6L + 4L + 24$$
$$= L^2 + 10L + 24$$

a) How does Grace go about drawing her pictures?

b) What do you think she says in her head to fill in the writing on the sides and inside the shapes?

c) Grace is using her method for multiplication to do all these questions, but not all the questions look like multiplications. Is it right for Grace to be treating them as multiplications?

d) Use Grace's method to draw rectangle pictures for the following expressions:

   i) $2x(x + 6)$

   ii) $a(2a + 3b)$

   iii) $(y + 6)(y + 2)$

8 a) Draw a rectangle picture for $x(x + 4)$ in the following cases:

   i)   If x is smaller than 4

   ii) If x is bigger than 4

   iii) If x is very large

   iv) If x is equal to 4

b) Compare your pictures with your classmates. Who has drawn the shape with the biggest area?

Turn to pages 20–22 of your workbook and try Workbook exercise 3.2.

9 Lauren is a student in Grace's class. She is puzzled:
'What I don't get is how you know that $x(x + 2)$ must be equal to $x^2 + 2x$?'

Grace draws her picture again to explain.

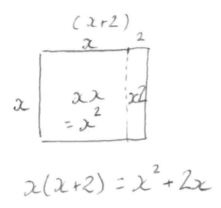

$$x(x+2) = x^2 + 2x$$

Grace explains:
'$x(x + 2)$ is one way to work out the area of the rectangle, like you're counting across the whole row. $x^2 + 2x$ is another way to work out the area where you've broken up the rows. It's the same rectangle so those answers must be the same.'

a) Use Grace's diagram to say how $x(x + 2)$ will work out the area.

b) Use Grace's diagram to say how you know that $x^2 + 2x$ will work out the same area.

c) Draw diagrams like Grace's to help you decide whether the following expressions are worth the same as each other or not:

i) $35 \times 107 = 3745$

ii) $31^2 = 901$

iii) $p(3p + 1) = 3p^2 + p$

iv) $3(a + b + c) = 3abc$

v) $x(x + 2y) = x^2 + 2yx$

vi) $5(3a + 7b - 1) = 15a + 35b - 5$

vii) $2y(3y + 6) = 6y^2 + 8y$

viii) $(L + 6)(L + 4) = L^2 + 10L + 24$

Perimeter and area

10 Look at the rectangle shown below.

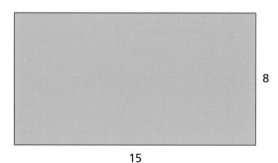

15

Sam said she worked out the area of this rectangle by doing 15 lots of 8.

Joel said he worked out the area of the rectangle by doing 8 lots of 15.

a) Where can you see 15 lots of 8 in the picture?

b) Where can you see 8 lots of 15 in the picture?

c) Explain why these answers must be the same.

d) Here are some ways to work out the perimeter of the shape:

   $15 \times 2 + 8 \times 2$ $2(15 + 8)$

   $15 + 8 + 15 + 8$ $8 + 15 + 8 + 15$

   Run your finger along the rectangle to show the 'journey' associated with each of these calculations.

e) Explain why the answers must be the same.

11 Some students were asked to find the perimeter of the shape shown below.

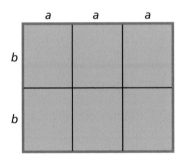

Here are some of the students' answers:

$$p = a + a + a + b + b + a + a + a + b + b$$

$$p = 3a \times 2 + 2b \times 2$$

$$p = b + 3a + b \times 2$$

$$p = 6a + 4b$$

$$p = 10ab$$

$$p = 2(2b + 3a)$$

a) Use your finger to draw round the 'journey' associated with each answer.

b) Decide whether each answer is correct or not.

c) Which is the neatest way of writing the perimeter?

d) Which journey does this come from?

e) Give two different ways of finding the area of this shape.

f) Use the picture to justify why $3a \times 2b$ must be equal to $6ab$.

12 Look at the shape shown below.

4a

5a

a) Find the perimeter of this shape in two different ways.

b) Find the area of the shape in two different ways.

 Turn to pages 23–25 in your workbook and complete Workbook exercise 3.3.

Expanding and factorising

13

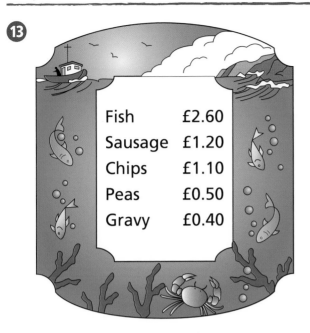

Fish	£2.60
Sausage	£1.20
Chips	£1.10
Peas	£0.50
Gravy	£0.40

Jane and Azim work in a chip shop. They have different ways of recording the orders that come in to the chip shop.

An order comes in for '5 lots of fish, chips and peas'.

This is what Jane writes on the order slip.

$5(f + c + p)$

This is what Azim writes on his order slip.

$5f + 5c + 5p$

a) Jane and Azim package the food according to the way they write the order down. How do you think Jane packages the food for this order?

b) Explain why $5(f + c + p)$ must mean the same as $5f + 5c + 5p$.

> The **expanded** version for working out
> this food order is $5f + 5c + 5p$.
> The **factorised** version for working out
> this food order is $5(f + c + p)$.

14 Look at the rectangle shown below.

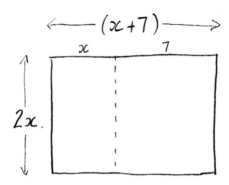

You can write down an expression for the area of this rectangle in different ways.

The **expanded** version for working out the area is $2x^2 + 14x$.

The **factorised** version for working out the area is $2x(x + 7)$.

a) Explain how you know that these areas must be worth the same amount.

b) The following expressions are in factorised form. Draw rectangle pictures to help you write them in expanded form.

    i) $p(p + 4)$

    ii) $2a(3a + 7)$

    iii) $x(4x + 2y + 7)$

    iv) $3b(b + c)$

When an expression is in expanded form, you can draw a rectangle picture to help you find the factorised form.

For example, to find the factorised form of $5x^2 + xy$:

- Draw a rectangle.
- Split it into two blocks, because there are two parts to the expression.
- Imagine that the inside areas are $5x^2$ and xy.
- What could the side lengths be?

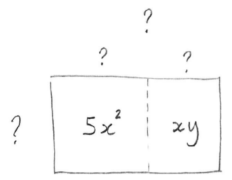

Finding possible side lengths helps you write the expression in a factorised form.
The factorised form of $5x^2 + xy$ is: $x(5x + y)$

15 **a)** Draw a rectangle picture to help you factorise $8ab + 14a$.

b) Draw a rectangle picture to help you factorise $20x + 12xy$.

 Turn to pages 26–28 of your workbook and do Workbook exercise 3.4. This gives you more practice at using a rectangle picture to help with factorising.

Using the 'lots of' strategy

Many people use the 'lots of' strategy to expand brackets. They think of it like this:

$4(3a + 2)$ means	4 lots of $(3a + 2)$
which is	$(3a + 2) + (3a + 2) + (3a + 2) + (3a + 2)$
which is	(4 lots of $3a$) + (4 lots of 2)
which is	$12a + 8$

16 **a)** Use the 'lots of' strategy to expand the brackets in the following expressions:

    i) $3(2x + 10)$

    ii) $2(3a + 4b)$

    iii) $4(3x - 1)$

    iv) $3(3y - 4) + 5y$

    v) $2(2p - 5q) + 4(10q - p)$

    vi) $5f + 2(f - g) + 4g$

b) Design six expressions similar to the ones in part **a)** for your neighbour to expand. When they have done them, check their work.

17 **a)** What happens when you use the 'lots of' strategy to expand $4a(3a + 2)$? Can you make sense of it?

b) Draw a rectangle picture to help you expand $4a(3a + 2)$.

Using the 'times by' strategy

Some people use the 'times by' strategy to expand brackets.
They think of it like this:

$4a(3a + 2)$ means $(4a$ times by $3a) + (4a$ times by $2)$

which is $12a^2 + 8a$

18 **a)** Use the 'times by' strategy to expand the following expressions:

   i) $t(t + 3)$ **ii)** $3b(b - 4)$

   iii) $2w(2w + 10v)$ **iv)** $3a(a + 5b - 7)$

   v) $x(x - 2y - 3)$ **vi)** $2(7c + 1) + 3(2c - 6)$

   vii) $x(x + 1) + 2x(x + 3)$ **viii)** $4d + d(2d - 1)$

  b) Design six expressions similar to the ones in part **a)** for your
      neighbour to expand. When they have done them, check their work.

19 Joel is trying to factorise $3ab - 9b$. He says: 'This looks like it might have
    come from b 'times by' something.

    His friend Sam thinks it has come from 3 'times by' something.

  a) Why does Joel say this?

  b) Why does Sam say this?

  c) Factorise $3ab - 9b$ as fully as possible.

20 Factorise the following where possible.

  a) $6x - 2y$ **b)** $8bc - 11ab$

  c) $4a + 10b - 12c$ **d)** $20c - 12cd$

  e) $5t^2 - 2t$ **f)** $7x^2 + 8y$

  g) $6p^2 + 1$ **h)** $8pq + 6qr$

21 **a)** Design five expressions, similar to the ones in **question 20**, which can
      be factorised.

  b) Design five expressions, similar to the ones in **question 20**, which
      cannot be factorised.

  c) Give all ten expressions (in a different order) to your neighbour for
      them to try to factorise.

Summary

In this chapter you have looked at the connection between multiplication and counting the number of squares in a rectangular grid.

If someone is asked what 24 × 37 means, they will often say 24 'lots of' 37.

If someone is asked what 24 × 37 looks like, they might say, for example, 24 piles with 37 counters in each.

The answer to 24 × 37 can be found by drawing a rectangle and imagining how to count the number of squares in that rectangle.

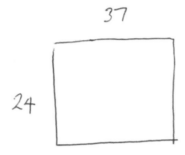

There are lots of ways you can count the number of squares in the rectangle, for example:

1 You can touch-count every one.

2 You can split the rectangle up into easy-to-count blocks.

Below are two ways of splitting the rectangle which give two ways of finding the answer to 24 × 37:

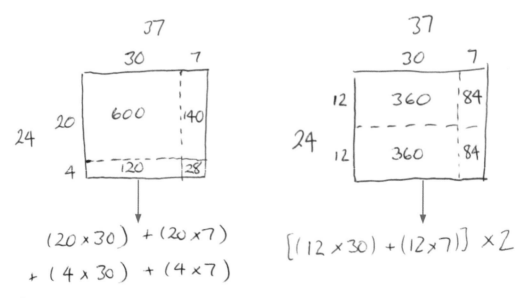

These ways are said to be 'equivalent'. This means the values are the same, but the method for working out the value is different.

In this chapter we used the rectangle to find equivalent ways of writing algebraic expressions.

For example: $3p(2p + q + 2)$

This really means $3p$ times $(2p + q + 2)$.

One way to work out $3p(2p + q + 2)$ can be to draw a rectangle and split it up:

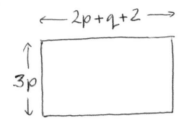 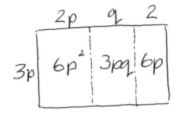

One way to find the area of this rectangle is to times the width by the length.

Another way is to find the area of the smaller blocks and add them together.

These two answers must be the same.

So: $3p(2p + q + 2) = 6p^2 + 3pq + 6p$

In maths, going from an expression in brackets to one without brackets is called **expanding**.

Turning a non-bracketed expression into one with brackets is called **factorising**.

As well as drawing rectangle pictures, you also looked at other methods for expanding and factorising. Through these methods you should be able to see that:

An expression such as: $2x(x + y) + 4y(x + 3)$

Can be **expanded** to: $2x^2 + 2xy + 4xy + 12y$

And **simplified** to: $2x^2 + 6xy + 12y$

And **factorised** to: $2(x^2 + 3xy + 6y)$

The honesty box

1　In West Park there's a Pitch and Putt golf course. In summer it's very busy and Bill the Park Keeper collects the money from people using it. However, in winter there aren't many people wanting to play so, instead, people have to put the exact money into an 'honesty box'. At the end of each day Bill collects the money from the box.

The Sports Council is keen to know how many children are playing golf. They want to encourage participation and hopefully find the Tiger Woods of the future.

Adults pay £3.50 to play and children pay £2.50.

Bill wants to know how many adults and how many children used the Pitch and Putt one day. At the end of the day there is £13.00 in the box. How many adults and how many children played that day?

2　On another day, there is £32.00 in the box. How many adults and how many children played on this day?

3　After a few more days, Bill thinks that there must a quicker way of finding out how many adults and how many children have played. He decides to make price lists, one for the cost of adults playing, the other for the cost of children playing.

Turn to page 29 of your workbook and complete the table of prices for Pitch and Putt in Workbook exercise 4.1.

4 Explain how Bill could use his lists to help him work out how many adults and how many children use the Pitch and Putt each day.

5 How much money would be in the box if eight adults and six children had used the Pitch and Putt during the day?

6 On the eighth day, £32.50 was in the box. Use the lists to work out how many adults and how many children used the Pitch and Putt that day.

7 Bill was still not satisfied with his method for finding out how many adults and children had played Pitch and Putt. He decided to put all the information into one table, a combination chart. This is the start of his combination chart:

The cost of combinations in £'s

Number of Children	0	1	2	3	4	5	6	7	8	9	10
10											
9											
8											
7											
6											
5	12.50	16.00	19.50	23.00							
4	10.00	13.50	17.00	20.50	24.00						
3	7.50	11.00	14.50	18.00	21.50						
2	5.00	8.50	12.00	15.50	19.00						
1	2.50	6.00	9.50	13.00	16.50						
0	0	3.50	7.00	10.50	14.00	17.50					

Number of Adults

a) Find 9.50 in the chart. What does this tell you?

b) What does 10.50 in the chart tell you?

 Turn to page 30 of your workbook and complete the rest of the combination chart for the Pitch and Putt prices in Workbook exercise 4.2.

8 **a)** Explain how Bill could use this chart to work out how many adults and how many children use the Pitch and Putt each day.

   b) On some days, after counting the money in the box, Bill wouldn't be sure how many adults and children had used the Pitch and Putt. Explain why he wouldn't always know.

9 While you were filling in the chart, you may have noticed some number patterns and used them to fill in the chart more quickly. For example, you may have noticed that as you went across you added on 3.50 (or £3.50) each time.

   a) What is the pattern as you move vertically up the chart?

   b) Why do we get this pattern?

10

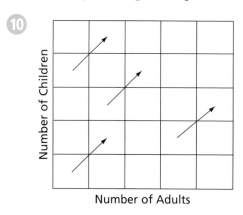

   Number of Adults

   a) What happens to the numbers in the chart when you move diagonally along the arrows shown above?

   b) What is happening to the number of adults and children when you move diagonally along the arrows?

11 **a)** In which direction would the arrows point to indicate one less adult and one more child? Mark this on page 29 of your workbook (**Workbook exercise 4.2**). Label this arrow **11 a**.

   b) What is the difference in price when this happens?

12 **a)** In which direction would the arrows point to indicate two more adults and one more child? Mark this on page 29 of your workbook (**Workbook exercise 4.2**). Label this arrow **12 a**.

   b) What is the price change this time?

Break time

13 At Kingswood Community School the teachers love their break-time drink. In the staffroom a lady makes the tea and coffee before break so that the thirsty teachers can grab a drink as soon as they come in. They pay for their drink by leaving the exact money in a saucer. A cup of coffee costs 25p. A cup of tea costs 18p. The tea lady wants to keep track of how much tea and coffee has been drunk so that she can order some more stock.

 Turn to page 31 of your workbook and fill in the combination table for the total cost of the different numbers of teas and coffees in Workbook exercise 4.3.

14 Explain how the tea lady can use the combination table to calculate the number of cups of tea and coffee sold.

15 On Monday, there was £1.90 on the saucer at the end of break. Use your combination table to work out how many cups of tea and how many cups of coffee had been bought.

16 On Tuesday, £2.54 was on the saucer at the end of break. Use your combination table to work out how many cups of tea and how many cups of coffee had been bought on that day.

17 On Wednesday, £2.40 was on the saucer at the end of break. However, Mr Johnson had paid for two teas and accidentally taken two coffees. Being very honest, Mr Johnson returns and puts the difference in price in the saucer.

a) How much extra money did Mr Johnson put in the saucer?

b) Mark with an arrow on your combination table the change in the total amount of money for that day.

c) Your arrow should go diagonally down two and across two to the right. Try this move in other places on the combination table. What do you notice? Why does this always happen?

18 a) Make up a story about what the following combination table could be used for.

b) How would you label the horizontal and vertical sides?

85	97	109	121	133	145
68	80	92	104	116	128
51	63	75	87	99	111
34	46	58	70	82	94
17	29	41	53	65	77
0	12	24	36	48	60

Pitch and Putt at North Park

19 Helen is the Park Keeper at North Park. She likes to set puzzles. Instead of telling people the price for adults and the price for children to play Pitch and Putt at North Park, she puts up this notice:

One adult and two children
costs £8.25

Two adults and one child
costs £9.75

a) It costs more for an adult to play Pitch and Putt than a child. How can you tell this from the notice?

b) How much more expensive is it for an adult?

20 a) What would be the cost for no adults and three children to play?

b) What is the cost for one child?

21 a) What would be the cost for three adults and no children to play?

b) What is the cost for one adult?

22 Make a copy of the combination table below. Fill in all the information from the park notice and **questions 20** and **21**.

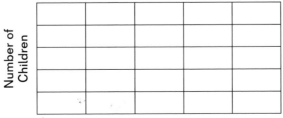

Number of Children

Number of Adults

The shop at North Park

23 Mr Johnson takes his form to play Pitch and Putt as an end of year treat. The children are in groups and each group wants to buy items from the shop. Mr Johnson decides it will be quicker and easier if he collects the orders from the groups and then buys everything together. These are the orders that he collects in his notebook:

Group	Golf balls	Caps	Umbrellas	Total cost (in £)
A	4	2	3	28
B	2	2	1	13
C	0	2	1	10
D	4	4	2	
E	2	4	2	
F	4	4	4	
G	1	1	1	
H	1	2	1	

Mr Johnson is in a hurry and only writes down the cost for the first three groups. However, he says that is enough information to work out the total cost for the other groups. Work out the cost for the other groups.

24 Use the notebook in **question 23** to work out the cost of:

a) a golf ball

b) a cap

c) an umbrella.

25 Mr Johnson uses his notebook again when he takes his form to the café.

The orders of the first three students are shown below. There is a £2.00 spending limit for each student. The rest of the class want to know the price of each item so they can get as much as possible for their £2.00.

Student	Crisps	Ice creams	Cans	Total cost (£)
1	1	0	1	1.20
2	0	1	1	1.70
3	1	1	0	1.30

a) Copy the table and make up some new price combinations.

b) Work out the price of each individual item.

c) Is there a way of spending exactly £2.00?

26 Harry and Lucas think that the ice cream van might be cheaper than the café. Harry bought one packet of crisps and two ice creams for £2.05. Lucas bought two packets of crisps and three ice creams for £3.30.

a) List this information in notebook form.

b) Work out some more combinations of ice creams and crisps and find their prices.

c) Are Harry and Lucas right? Is the ice cream van cheaper for ice creams and crisps?

More chocolate!

27 Harry decides to buy some snacks for his friends. He buys two Swirls and three Beasts. It costs him £4.70.

He writes down $2S + 3B = 470$. This is called an equation.

Lucas also buys snacks for his friends. He spends £2.90 on the following:

Write down the cost of Lucas's snacks as an equation.

28 Harry records his purchases in a combination table and in notebook form.

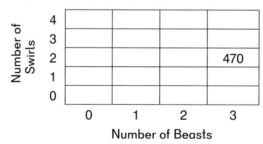

Swirls	Beasts	Cost
2	3	470

Turn to page 32 of your workbook (Workbook exercise 4.4) and record Lucas's purchases in the combination table and in the notebook.

29 a) Use the combination table and the notebook to work out other price combinations.

b) Use the combination table and the notebook to work out the cost of a Swirl and the cost of a Beast.

30 More people go to buy snacks for their friends. Samit buys three Kat Kats and one Mounty for £2.40. Julie buys two Kat Kats and two Mounties for £2.60.

£2.40

£2.60

a) Write these purchases as equations.

b) Use the combination table or the notebook method to work out the cost of a Kat Kat and the cost of a Mounty.

31 Here are two more equations:

$3L + 2M = 98$

$L + M = 38$

The numbers 98 and 38 could represent lengths, weights, prices or whatever you want them to be.

a) Make up a story to fit these equations.

b) Find the value of L and the value of M.

Summary

In this chapter you've seen that the notebook and the combination table are good ways of getting an overview of the information in a problem.

Many problems involve quantities such as price, weight and length. One way to describe these problems is by using an equation.

For example, if three rubbers and one pencil cost 48p and one rubber and two pencils cost 56p, we could use a notebook or a combination table to find the cost of each individual item. This is how you could begin:

Notebook

Combination Table

Rubbers	Pencils	Cost
3	1	48
1	2	56

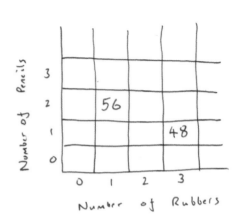

If you let R represent the price of one rubber and P represent the price of one pencil, the equations would be $3R + P = 48$ and $1R + 2P = 56$.